OVERCOMING MY VAGINISMUS

A definite guide to cure vaginismus without using dilators

By Maria Gonzalez

INDEX OF CONTENTS

Who am I?

Hello, dear reader, I'd like to introduce myself in the first place. I'm not a therapist or a psychologist. In fact, the first review of the original Spanish version of this book was an attack from a sexologist, simply because I'm not a professional adviser... Oh well, I'm "just" a woman suffering from vaginismus during all my life... For many years I searched for a solution, in vain. I know how you feel, I know you're reading this book because you really want to give it a solution. Maybe you tried everything or maybe not. Be it as it may, I hope you find here a friend's voice who can help you. I really hope so.

I don't mean to be a substitute for a doctor, I only hope you can take your first step to get out of this situation. The first step is the most important, trust me. I decided to tell my story because there's not much help out there from a personal point of view. I could only read about women telling how happy or unhappy they felt, but they never explained how they solved the problem or which was the precise reason not to solve it. I know it's an embarrassing issue, invisible in most cases, so I just want to add some helpful information. I'll try to be clear and talk to you as if we were close friends. I never spoke of this to anyone, so it's helpful for me too. So, there we go.

When did my vaginismus start?

I'll tell you how that thing called vaginismus started for me. Maybe this is familiar to you or maybe not, but I'm sure the problem has always a reason behind, and the main reason is this: disinformation. I had no idea about my genital zone when I was a little girl. I remember a basic drawing in a school book when I was 10 years old. The vagina was depicted like a narrow duct. That's how I learned we supposedly had a sort of duct down there. Well, three years later, I was 13 and tried to use a tampon for the first time. It was summer and I wanted to go to a swimming pool. So I bought the tampons, read the instructions and locked in the bathroom.

In those days tampons were just a piece of round hard paper with cotton inside. I thought the instructions were confusing: try to relax yourself and insert it towards the lower part of your back. I just thought it had to be easier, something like locating the entrance to the duct I had seen in my school book. I took one tampon and put it where I thought my vagina could be. Then I pushed but... it seemed there was no such a duct. I pushed again, not knowing what spot I was pressing, and I just felt I was running into a closed wall. It was a weird and unpleasant experience. I had never played with my vagina before, although I knew well where my clitoris was (not that I had ever looked at it) and I had experienced orgasms on rubbing it. I didn't need to play with my vagina to feel pleasure, so I didn't know how it worked, or how it looked or anything. I gave up trying to use tampons and didn't try again for a while. Sanitary napkins were my best choice, and besides, those days were always painful for me so I had no energy to swim.

I didn't have a boyfriend then and wasn't interested in sex either. When I was a teenager there was no internet and I didn't speak of my problem with anybody, so I forgot about my vagina for the next three years.

My problem getting worse

I was 16 and I thought I couldn't go on like that. It was summer again and I went to the beach for a few days. Just then I had my period and I wanted to swim. My periods were so painful that my doctor told me to take contraceptive pills to solve it. I was feeling much better than in the past so I told to myself I really had to start using tampons.

It was a big step, the kind of step we take when we have an important reason. It can be just swimming or maybe getting pregnant. Or maybe we're just so tired of the situation, of feeling there's something abnormal in our lives. The feeling of "I want to be like the rest" is a powerful motivation too. So in my case, trying to use tampons again was a positive step, but unfortunately, I didn't do it right for the same old reason: disinformation. I took the tampons and went to the bathroom. I took a deep breath and tried to relax. I put the tampon close to my vagina. I thought it couldn't be so difficult, all the girls seemed to do it effortlessly.

The tampon was better than the first I had tried to

insert three years back, softer and with an applicator. My own bloody flow acted like a lubricant, and somehow, the tampon began to get inside a bit. I felt happy for it meant an improvement, but at the same time, I didn't like the sensation. Feeling that thing inside was uncomfortable. I felt suddenly indisposed, even dizzy. I know it may sound ridiculous but I had to sit on the floor out of fear to faint. It was so disturbing, I just wanted to get it out. Then I remembered the instructions: if you feel it, then it's not in its right place; you need to push it further... Great. So the tampon wasn't in nor wasn't out, so I pulled it out, although my vagina was kind of stuck in shock. I pulled hard and it was... oh so unpleasant! I know it now, but not then: my vagina was contracting so that's why I could feel so intensely what was inside.

It was such a horrible experience I promised myself to forget about my vagina forever. But I must say it was a positive step after all. It was the first time I did some improvement, and I used that starting point when I faced the problem again. But many years came to pass before that, exactly 20 years...

Two decades without sex

Obviously, I couldn't plan on doing normal things like having a partner, getting pregnant, etc. So I spent my time studying first, then working, being with friends, etc., and sex didn't exist for me, just masturbation. 20 years is so much time and we can't be young forever. I don't know if I was fooling myself, thinking I wasn't interested in boys, or maybe I thought I was hopelessly defective. Anyway, years went by and I only fell in love in my imagination a couple of times. I had only a few short real dates. I had my first kiss when I was 18, and hated the experience. His breath was disgusting and I didn't like feeling his wetness on my lips. I never saw him again. My next kiss was when I was 35, and luckily it was a pleasant moment this time. But my sexual activity was non-existent.

My life was quite normal in the rest of fields. I worked, hanged out with friends and so on, I felt I could do anything except using my vagina. Internet was already a companion in my life and I had learned many things thanks to online information. It was amazing and comforting when I found out vaginismus was a problem for many women. Penis dysfunction is a topic broadly discussed and known, but it seems as if women don't have any problem in the intercourse. Maybe it's a huge problem affecting many women, but if they don't talk about it, nobody knows. I must admit I never sought medical help. And when the guy of my second kiss knew why I couldn't have sex with him after a couple of tries, I had to endure his rejection and mockery. It was hard and frustrating. But let's start with the first place where I found some comfort and "company": internet.

Vaginismus on the Internet

While I looked for information about vaginismus I found forums, I read everything I could about the issue, I learned about the methods to overcome it, but I had the feeling they were useless in my case. The truth is, I do believe those methods don't work in the beginning. I mean, the treatment kits... What the...! Who could think of such a ridiculous way of solving the problem of "being narrow" by inserting something into a place where obviously it doesn't fit in? I think it's not a method for starters. But they try to sell it as the best and only way to overcome vaginismus. Sad and absurd, in my opinion. It's just a piece of cold plastic, it has little to do with a real penis. Ok, many women play in solitude with that kind of stuff, but I insist, it's not the perfect way to start overcoming vaginismus. It's a strange object, you need something more... familiar, as your own fingers.

Also, those kits are expensive and they can make you feel as if you needed orthopedic objects to turn you into a normal woman. The solution is not inserting things in a narrow place, the solution is getting the narrowness disappear, as I'll explain later.

There are therapists solving the problem, or so they say. I don't mean to attack them, as I never tried with any of them, but it's such an embarrassing issue and they're just strangers after all, so it's complicated. And I'm sure not all the therapists are the right ones for all the women with vaginismus. It's a physical problem, but also a psychological one, and if you're feeling embarrassed in front of a stranger, it's not a positive thing for your cure.

So, I just kept reading about vaginismus on the Internet from time to time. Until I had my first boyfriend and I couldn't hide it any longer. But first, I have to tell you a couple of critical moments.

Gynecological check

Since I had no sexual activity, I thought I didn't need checking. But my periods got very irregular and I found a small lump on my breast, so my doctor sent me to a gynecological check. When I got there, to my surprise, they told me to undress completely. First, they asked me a few questions, one of them concerning my sexual activity. I said I was 27 but I was still a virgin. We were in a hospital, the doctor was a woman and there was a male medicine student with us. She didn't change her expression on hearing me, but the boy was clearly trying hard not to giggle. She told him to leave us alone for the next step, thankfully, which was inserting one finger in my anus and touching my ovaries through my belly with her another hand. After that embarrassing moment, which ironically wasn't a big physical issue for me, she sent me, half-dressed as I was, to another room to check my breasts. I had to walk beside the young student who was with a couple of persons whom I didn't dare look at. However, I noticed they all looked at me intently and I felt sure my virginity confession had spread quickly.

Thank God, the lump on my breast was of no importance and the problem with my period was fixed with pills. But 5 years later I had to get back for the same reason. This time the doctor was a man. He also learned I was a virgin and asked two nurses to stay with us for the check. I felt even more embarrassed than the first time. I couldn't see anything with that sort of sheet over my legs but I sensed he touched the outer part of my vagina, so I complained. He showed me a large cotton swab and said, in a surprised tone, he had only touched me with that thing. The nurses kept telling me to relax, at least my anus... but I was completely tense, so he stopped trying and we got to his desk. He was writing for a long time. I felt uneasy, angry, I just wanted to leave. He looked at me and asked me if there was something wrong with me. I answered I didn't like to go to any medical place, which is quite true, and he didn't ask anything else. When I remember this, I think his attitude was unforgivable. I mean, he didn't give me any advice nor did he try to help me in any way, maybe by sending me to a therapist. Oh well, I guess that's how these things work... But the worst was yet to come: my third gynecological check.

I must explain first, I could insert two or three fingers in my vagina by that time. But even so, it was a horrible experience. I was able to get as far as inserting those fingers all by myself, and if such a serious case as mine can be cured, I assure you, every woman must have a cure too. We all have a vagina and we can learn how to take control over it. But let's get back to my third gynecological check. Although I was relaxed about the lump on my breast, I wanted to check it again in the future. My doctor said I needed a cytology first. I didn't understand why, as I didn't have any sexual activity and my period was fine. But she told me it was a routine for every woman. So I tried to get ready for the moment, a couple of months later, by doing my vagina exercises. I had to stretch it like never before so they could insert the speculum.

The day came and I explained I was a virgin, so they had to use the smallest speculum, the one they used for little girls, the nurse told me. I took my position, such a vulnerable one as you know, and a young female doctor came in the room. To make things worse, an old lady opened the door just then: she

16

couldn't find her doctor's office. She couldn't see me from her position and I was concentrating hard on controlling my nerves, but the nurse got angry and told the old lady to get out of there quickly. Then my doctor said, here we go, and she inserted the speculum all of a sudden and fast. It was not so hard after all, it was like inserting my three fingers, but then... then she opened the speculum and I felt my vagina stretching beyond any earlier point. Then I totally felt the speculum in there, it was annoying, so I started to shout "get it out!" almost in tears. It was like... I felt they were attacking me. She knew I was a virgin but she wasn't careful nor respectful. Maybe I could have done better at a slower pace, or maybe there was no possible way for me to feel comfortable because that was too much for my vagina. I was sobbing and saying "oh get it out" and I'm sure I didn't get dizzy because I was too angry to faint.

The doctor said she couldn't stop because she was spotting my cervix just then. She rubbed something in there and I felt a new pain, just below my belly button. It was so weird, feeling the pain in a part of my body which I didn't know it existed until then. The nurse started to laugh (can you believe it?) and showed me the normal speculum. The doctor told the nurse "thank God doctor such isn't here today, he's so rough". I couldn't believe my ears. Two medical women being so rude with a female virgin! I dressed up quickly and when I opened the door, all the women who were waiting for their turn looked at me in surprise or full of curiosity or I don't know what they were thinking, but I was sure everybody had heard me screaming loud.

Losing my fear to my own vagina

After my second gynecological check, the one with the male doctor, I realized a couple of things. It was not only that my muscles tightened when somebody tried to touch me down there. Even when I tried to touch myself, I couldn't do it! It was even painful. The day I had half inserted the tampon was turning into a fading memory. I had to admit I had a phobia concerning my vagina, and it was getting worse every day. The second thing I realized was this: I was always, always, contracting my vagina. It was something unconscious. Those muscles were tightened, all the time.

Overcoming vaginismus is not an easy journey. Sometimes I was able to insert a couple of fingers in my vagina but if I stopped doing so for a while, I was at the starting point again. It's logical, if you stop training, you lose an ability. Although you don't lose it completely, your body has a sort of inner memory. But the thing is, I was contracting my vagina muscles all the time, and in doing so, I was training the opposite way to overcome vaginismus! So I started solving my first problem. I had to be able to touch myself and not feel any pain.

When my periods got irregular, my hormones were kind of crazy, so I got hairy legs and forearms. That was another reason for avoiding boys. So when I could save some money, I chose laser hair removal to solve my hairy problem. That's how I learned something that helped me a lot on my first step. When you're trying to cure any kind of phobia, the process starts by losing your fear little by little. My first fear was touching the entrance to my vagina. Then I remembered the laser hair removal and the lubricant anesthesia they used on my skin. I read about the product and it could be used for easy genital surgery too. So that's what I did: I put some anesthesia on the zone so I could touch it without fear. It worked, it really worked.

This kind of ointment is easy to purchase, and you can even use it inside your vagina on a little dose. But if you don't like the idea, you can try other ways to decrease your sensibility there, for example: using ice cubes wrapped in a cloth, or if you prefer, using something warm, like hot water in the shower. Just take a bath and try to change from cold to hot, and try different levels of intensity with the jet. Maybe you don't need to do this (I did needed it) but you won't lose your time if you learn about your sensibility down there, if you learn about your own body, because that's the key in my opinion: information, so you can stop being afraid of what you don't know.

When you're able to touch yourself, try to do it softer and harder, to check your own reactions, and little by little you will be able to control your own body. I must confess, my healing idea was precisely this: controlling my body. I felt so ridiculous when I realized I had been leaving out of my control something that belonged to me, something that was a part of me, something that was... me after all. I realized I was betraying myself.

But, please, I don't want you to feel guilty, we're not guilty for the disinformation. Nobody told us about these things or they did it the wrong way. I just started to see things clear, I believed there was a cure and it was within my reach. I don't know why I was afraid to touch my vagina, maybe it was because of my catholic education, or my family, or my shyness, or simply my disinformation. After I lost my fear to touch the entrance to my vagina, I tried to take another step. The problem is, I rushed again and I didn't do it right. So you must never rush, this is important.

Losing my virginity with myself

Maybe someone may think my problem wasn't vaginismus, as I was a virgin and that is all. But I tell you, when I lost my virginity, the problem was still there. By the way, I had had sex before losing my virginity. I mean, sex is not only the intercourse, and I felt I wasn't a complete virgin even if I couldn't insert anything in my vagina. It was a psychological sensation, and it was important for me to feel that way, because I felt psychologically ready to stop being a physical virgin. I don't mean to change your view about virginity, in case you're still a virgin. It shouldn't be an important issue in my opinion. A woman may insert things in her vagina and not have intercourse with any man. Virginity supposedly means a penis getting into a vagina for the first time. In our case, I think trying to do that is a wrong idea. We don't need to suffer any pain, we shouldn't bleed, we shouldn't... sacrifice. And I'm not talking about vaginismus now, I mean all the women should have the power to control their own vaginas and not let any man take control of it, especially the first time. I don't think it's a romantic thing at all.

This book is not about our ability to have intercourse, to begin with. It's about our interaction with our own vagina and its ability to get stretched. Also, I don't think vaginismus really exists, it's only we have a non-trained vagina. So I think vaginismus is a (temporary) state of the vagina in which it doesn't allow anything to enter, or doesn't stretch wide enough for intercourse.

I'm telling you everything that happened to me because I hope you can use my helpful experiences and avoid my same mistakes. Now I'll tell you a big dangerous mistake. When I was able to insert a finger for the first time after so many years, I felt so happy and proud of me. In fact, that first finger is the key to your recovery. What comes after is not so hard once you can do it. If you can do that, you'll do the rest, step by step. But you must be patient and not hurry up, as I did.

First, I'll tell you how I inserted a finger quite easily. It's useful to use a mirror. The vagina is so hidden and you can't see it by yourself, so it's normal we don't know how it looks like or how it works, unlike it happens with a penis. Lay back on a comfortable position and place the mirror leaning on a cushion, book, etc., so you can use your hands freely. Use nice lighting or a lantern. Then open the outer lips of your vulva. Relax yourself and use the right position to watch everything easily. You don't need to be very flexible or open your legs much. The entrance to the vagina is beyond the inner lips of your vulva, so you need to separate them enough to look inside.

Every vagina is different, so maybe your hymen is intact and you can't see the entrance to your vagina. But trust me, it's there. The proof is, your blood comes out of there in every period. So, if you can't see any hole, try to push as if you were to poop. That will cause the entrance to widen a bit. When you see that little hole, even if it's really small, you'll have a sort of thread in your hands and after that, you'll start to pull that thread until you're in total control of your vagina. It's not essential to see the hole, but it helps a lot. Either if you can see it or not, the main step is using your finger now. And, please, don't use it dry! Use your own saliva or some watery lubricant. If you're properly lubricated, that can make miracles, trust me. It's what happened to me when I used my first tampon, because my own blood acted like a lubricant. Maybe you feel like trying to insert your finger during your period. I never tried to do it in those days, because my vagina was swollen and sore, but maybe you don't have the same problem.

When you're ready, lubricated and relaxed, the next step is inserting your finger. When I tried to insert my first tampon, what I actually did was bumping into my vaginal wall. I had no idea where the entrance to my vagina was, and I didn't understand the part about pointing towards the lower part of my back. The vagina is not a straight duct, to begin with, it's a bit bent right in the entrance (great, yeah...). Using your own finger is very useful for two reasons: it's a part of your own body instead of a strange object, and also, you can bend it the way you need. For me, the best way to insert it is from behind. I put a hand on my buttock and then it goes down towards the entrance of my vagina. When your finger is into, or near, the hole of your vagina, point to the rectus direction and push gently. That's my best way to get the right angle.

If you touch yourself gently, beginning with the outer part, it's just a matter of time you get to touch your vagina in the inner part too. That's how I started to take control of my vagina. It was my healing idea, and I hope it's yours too. You have to control it, don't let it control your life. Also, the vagina is just a muscle, a bit different to the rest and it's around a cavity. But, being a muscle, it may change its behavior after massage and training, and that's the key: training your vagina. The good news is, no matter how long it's been closed, it will respond to your training. Mine had been closed for decades, so your case can't be much worse.

The first time you try to push your vaginal wall, to push that muscle, you're afraid it hurts, and the truth is, it hurts. It's logical, it's something new you never did before. It's like starting to run without a previous warm-up: your legs hurt, your muscles get hard, you feel as if needles were into your skin... So it's something new and you're nervous, even if you're trying to relax, and that makes things worse.

They say vaginismus is just a psychological problem, and it's not true, but it's not a lie either. There's a psychological part, because we have power in our minds. If you think you can do something, you do it. If you think you can't, you don't do it. In both cases, it's what you think, not the reality. I don't mean to jump out of the window and fly, you know what I mean. Most of women can use their vaginas, so you can do it too. But first, yours needs some training. That's all.

You have to work on your body and you have to work on your mind. You have to think: maybe it hurts, but it's not agony, and the next time I won't feel so much pain.

When I could insert my finger easily several times, I tried with two fingers. Then I tried with three. And one morning, I woke up and I felt my vagina was... wide. The night before I had an orgasm touching my clitoris. It was amazing and I never felt anything like that again. My vagina was wide by itself! I was very relaxed, it was my first day of holiday for a long time, and the miracle happened. And then I forgot I had to take it easy and made a mistake.

I had this kind of a cylinder resembling a penis, it was part of a set to curl my hair. It was soft and as thick as two of my fingers together. It was flat at the tip, with a wrinkled plastic piece there. I had a sudden idea. I could insert it in my vagina, it seemed the right time to use something different instead of my fingers. So I stood up and did it. It got in easily, but I did it too fast and didn't remember the vagina had an end, so the wrinkled tip got to the delicate cervix. It was painful, my muscles contracted and I felt them closing hard against the cylinder. I felt dizzy, like it happened with my first tampon, and I pulled it out fast. It was... bloodstained. I'll never know if it was because my hymen had broken or if the cylinder had done some harm to my cervix. That day I was bleeding until afternoon. It was slight bleeding, like on the last day of the period. That's how I lost my virginity with myself.

Somehow, I felt happy to be alone when it happened. If I would have been with a man using his penis... the idea is disgusting to me, honestly. But that kind of bloody story is what many women experience, unfortunately. Also, if you consider you're losing something when you lose your virginity, maybe it's what causes part of your vaginismus. It can be an unconscious fear, I think. However, if that's your case, you should think virginity is not something you lose, it's just you're doing something for the first time, and more accurately, you win something: experience and sexual freedom.

I think the hymen can be one of the reasons for vaginismus, but you can stretch it little by little instead of breaking it all of the sudden, like it happens many times, unfortunately. In my case, I was a virgin because I couldn't have intercourse, and I didn't have intercourse because I was a virgin. It's a damn circle, but you can solve it by yourself. Thanks to my advice, you don't need any man to solve it.

My first sexual experience

After my experience with the cylinder, I waited for some months before training my vagina again. I thought I was fully ready for intercourse. I was over 30 when I had my first boyfriend. It was around that era and I didn't tell him anything about my vagina. I didn't want to focus on that, I just wanted to be "normal". So one day he took me to his house and I was curious about how things could be with him. We had only kissed a few times before. That day we got into bed and had oral sex, both of us. Then he tried to insert his finger. I didn't expect it. He was rough, I guess he thought women like it that way... and it was painful. So I didn't feel like trying intercourse. I told him I wasn't relaxed enough and we did other things. At least I had a nice orgasm that day. But I knew I wasn't ready for intercourse at all. And I have to say something at this point.

The good part of being alone with my own sexuality for so long was I knew myself well. My pleasure belonged to me, I didn't depend on any man for that. I didn't feel forced to do what was supposedly normal. I had never needed intercourse to have my orgasms. In fact, the vagina is not our pleasure point but our clitoris. The vagina is meant for giving birth, of course, and you must use it if you want to have children. But don't you believe the only way of feeling pleasure is by inserting a penis in your vagina. That's only what everybody wants you to believe, especially men, and it's just a wrong idea that causes anxiety and stress to both partners.

That man wasn't stupid (just an asshole...) so he soon realized I was a virgin. He laughed at me and I broke with him, of course. You have to respect yourself and demand respect and understanding from any man. If you've never had an orgasm by yourself, I advise you to do it. If your religion tells you it's a dirty thing, then at least you should be able to touch your vulva, like you can touch any other part of the rest of your body.

But I don't want to focus on sex, although it's a related topic. You're trying to control your own body and from then on, you'll decide what you prefer. But if you can't choose, that's a limitation for you. That's why I kept on trying to fight against my vagina muscles. Before I continue, let's talk about vaginal anatomy.

You have to know your own vagina

You can find a lot of information about this on the Internet, but there aren't many good images, so there we go. The outer part of the vagina is the vulva, there we have the outer lips and the inner lips. Maybe your inner lips can be seen from outside the outer lips: don't worry, it's quite usual. The clitoris is just under the inner lips, on the upper side. Very close, there's a little hole to piss. If you open your inner lips, you should see the entrance to your vagina.

The hymen, in case you have it, is like a ring. It doesn't look the same in every woman, but it's like a weaker kind of skin, if compared to the vagina walls. It's like the inner part of your mouth, sort of. The thing is, it can get stretched and torn. Some elastic hymens can stretch to let a penis insert and later they get back to their previous state. On the contrary, some hymens are so tough that they need surgery to remove them. Usually, it bleeds if it stretches too sudden, because it tears. In my case, I never bled again after inserting that cylinder, I guess my hymen stretched gradually afterwards if some remaining part was left.

Beyond the hymen zone, which is the narrowest part of the vagina too, we get to another part. There, between the vagina and the belly, we have the pubic bone. You can press from the outside above your vulva so you'll know where it is. The inner part of the bone is like a spongy fabric, it's kind of wrinkled, and the G-spot is over there. If you touch it, your orgasm will be strong and quick. The first time I inserted three fingers deep down, I had one of those.

The rest of that zone is similar. The vagina is not flat, it has sort of rings, and they expand when the vagina opens. When I started stretching my vagina, it was easier for me to press towards the back, to the rectus direction. You have to look for the part you can stretch more easily. Beyond that area, we have the deepest part of the vagina. It's narrower there again, which is logical due to the lack of use. The muscles are quite tough there. But, like it happens with any other muscle, they get softer with a massage. You don't need to get so deep at first and your fingers won't reach there easily. At the end of the vagina, we have the cervix. It's the hole connecting with the uterus and it opens when you give birth. It's a delicate area, as I learned on my cytology, and it may hurt if the penis pushes it. Beyond the cervix, you can't insert anything by yourself, so don't panic if your tampon gets too inside. Just relax and get it out, it can't get lost inside your body.

Primary and secondary vaginismus

Maybe you know the difference, but let's explain this too. The primary vaginismus happens when you could never insert anything in your vagina before. The secondary vaginismus happens when you could do it in the past, but you can't do it from a certain point. You may think the secondary case is hard to believe, it's weird to step back once you can control your vagina, right? But if you have a traumatic experience, you can easily get to the starting point. The good thing of having used your vagina in the past is you have an important base to use in your recovery. If you could do it in the past, you'll be able to do it in the future.

Primary and secondary vaginismus are similar but different. It's like training for the Olympic Games for the first time opposed to getting back to training after an injury. The two of them are complicated situations, but you can overcome both, of course.

You are the owner of your body

I think it's important to stress this concept. Maybe you decided to avoid intercourse for whatever the reason. You can be heterosexual or homosexual or even asexual. Maybe you're a strict catholic. Maybe you're married or maybe you promised yourself to stay single forever. Maybe you're willing to get married or get divorced or have more sexual activity or have less. My point is, no matter what your present situation is and what your future plans are, the important thing is: don't let anybody tell you what you must or must not do. If you're reading this book because you want to please your man and be "normal" or if deep down you don't like him to the point of having intercourse, don't feel any pressure. It's your life and it's your body, you can control your vagina for the satisfaction of it, not because someone tells you so.

I tell you this because sometimes I trained my vagina beyond its limit, for the fear of feeling a weirdo with the man I was dating. And the sad part is, they were men of no importance at all in my life. I also made the mistake of confessing my vaginismus to the wrong man and I regretted it afterwards. It's okay not to hide it, at the right time with the right person, but there's no need to spread the news. I repeat, don't run, don't take the next step before controlling the former one, don't do it for any man, nor even for that special man who truly deserves you. In fact, you must not force yourself for that special man, because sometimes your vaginismus becomes the vaginismus of him and you. Let's talk about them next.

Your partner in the vaginismus of "both of you"

My modest intention is covering all the different cases of vaginismus. I read online many stories of women with this problem, most of them worried about not "passing the test" in their relationships. Maybe you feel the same way too, you may feel you're betraying your partner because you love him and you think it's unfair to deprive him of such intimate moments. Well, let me tell you, he chose you as his partner, so he should get involved in your problems, the same way you would, or he shouldn't make things worse at least.

I remember a certain testimony, unusual and infrequent, by a man concerning his partner's vaginismus. It was so moving, it almost made me cry. He was so understanding and kind. He said he'd wait for how long she needed, with no pressure, because she was the love of his life. Isn't it amazing? That should be the normal reaction, that's the attitude your partner should have. Please, don't try to overcome your vaginismus for any other person, no matter how much you love him. Do it for yourself and because you want to expand your sexual horizon.

I already told you about the first man who knew I was a virgin. He just laughed at me and thought I was a liar. He couldn't believe it, as I was so "old". Other men never knew it, and some had a suspicion, but I never fully told it to anyone. Until I met him.

I thought he was worthy of my efforts. Maybe I should train harder my vagina muscles, I thought. However, I didn't speed up. I didn't want to betray my decision of doing it only for myself. And he didn't add any pressure. Obviously, he wanted to go further and would be delighted to do so. Fortunately, he was open-minded and we enjoyed much, not focusing on the intercourse.

Your brain can betray you and I'll tell you why. When I was single, I felt totally freedom to train my vagina and I didn't think I did it for anybody. But if I met a man, deep down I felt I was exercising for him. The key is thinking correctly. Maybe you can find an extra reason in pleasing your man, but don't focus on that, and don't let him turn it into a stressing issue. Don't forget: it's your body, it's your mind.

Maybe you're a man reading this in search of help for your partner. Good for you. But be gentle, don't use this information to press her. Just try to understand what her vaginismus means. She doesn't refuse you, or it doesn't have to be the first explanation coming to your mind. Maybe that was her problem in the past with another man, so try to prove you're not all alike. If you're the first boy she has intimacy with, you need extra patience. But it'll be a magic moment when she can enjoy naturally her vagina by your side.

In my experience, the idea of surrendering to someone who could hurt me, even he didn't mean to do so, was terrifying. Once you're in control of your vagina, the solution to that fear is being in charge of the intercourse, at least on the first occasions. I hope your partner is intelligent and kind enough to let you do it. If it helps you and he wants to, you may tie his hands. Or maybe it's enough for you to put your body on his, so he can't push and you can move aside if he does. When you're ready to do it, after relaxing your vagina alone, or by his side but not using his penis, you can imagine you're doing your lonely exercises, only this time using a part of his body too.

Between your exercises using your fingers and the moment of using his penis, you could try using some object, if you like. I don't mean those huge pieces of plastic so terrifying at first sight, but something like a small vibrating bullet, as thick as your lipstick. It's like a finger and you can use it to massage your vagina walls, and to get used to have something strange inside.

I want to give you some helpful hint to use it with your partner. When you can insert a couple of fingers, you can do this exercise. Insert one finger and stretch your vagina a little, the way I'll explain later. Then, ask him to insert his finger between your finger and the gap. Or even better, guide his finger with your other hand, so there are no unpleasant surprises when he gets to the entrance of your vagina. Then, get your finger out and leave his inside. It's a simple and gradual way to get comfortable in that situation and you'll prevent him from "rummaging" down there.

The most important and difficult part when you're exercising alone is inserting your first finger. And when you're using a penis, the key part is locating the right spot and the right angle, so it won't be like colliding into a wall. On the first moments, you have to stretch your vagina alone or beside him, before inserting the penis. But let me tell you this. The intercourse is supposedly fun because both of you feel the friction. That is, your vagina will never be like a chewing gum where a penis can enter without you feeling a thing, because, in that case, you'll be in the opposite trouble. Some women have to train their vagina to tighten it, by contracting the muscles consciously. The training is for avoiding the pain in our vaginas, but it'll still be firm enough so as to allow the pleasurable intercourse, the same as it happens when you rub your clitoris. And the reason why you feel pleasure in the intercourse is because your clitoris is bigger than we can see and it's also inside your vagina.

At first, you'll only be able to let the tip of the penis in. That part of the penis is a bit flexible and round, so that makes it easier for adjusting to your entrance. Also, it usually is the narrowest part of the penis, although every penis is different. You can rub your clitoris and the entrance to your vagina with his penis, using natural or artificial lubrication, before you try to get further. In short, it's the same process you did alone, starting by massaging the outer part and then relaxing the inner part. When you relax all your body, you'll be aroused by his presence and that will cause your vagina to get wet and widen by itself too.

Let's break psychological taboos

Vaginismus is partly a physical limitation and partly a wrong psychological attitude. It's not all on your mind, as some people say, nor is it all purely physical. For years, I was advancing and taking steps back, until I found my healing idea. I was so tired of feeling abnormal about my vagina, and then I read something I can't remember where. It was like the last piece of a puzzle to help me face the problem. In my case, the healing idea was this: I wanted and I could control my body, the same as I had achieved many other things in life. I was not as young as other women who didn't have vaginismus but my overall experience in life was helpful too.

Let's review some wrong ideas we all have some time, which are toxic for overcoming vaginismus. And we'll see why they're all wrong ideas.

-There's no room for anything in there

You know that's totally untrue. However, you get to that conclusion because you feel you're different and abnormal. But there are no narrow vaginas, only non-trained vaginas.

-It will be painful

Human nature is wise. If you feel pain on trying the intercourse or inserting a tampon, your vagina just tells you it isn't ready. Ok, it hurts when it hurts, but that doesn't mean it will always hurt. And if you feel the pain, just stop and try another day.

-I actually want to continue being a virgin

You're not someone special for being a virgin. Some women are born without a hymen. You can have sexual activity without having intercourse. If your vagina is narrow at its entrance, it's just a transient situation. You don't have to "keep yourself pure" for anybody. It's useless to focus on that, no matter what your social circle or your religion tells you. This is only about you and a muscle of your body. If you look at it that way, virginity is just a ridiculous concept.

-I actually don't feel desire for my partner

You have to be very sincere with yourself on this topic. Maybe it's just fear to get hurt or maybe you don't actually like him enough. You may feel unconsciously rejection for him and you can't hide it in such an intimate moment. If that's your case, you may try therapy to save your relationship, or you can consider seriously a break-up. However, don't let any relationship damage your progress with your vagina. You can train it with or without a partner, and in both cases you'll do it for yourself, to be the owner of your own body. From that point on, you just decide if you want to share your body with someone or how far you want to get with him.

-It's too soon/ It's too late

I forgot about my vagina for years and I regretted later on. Even if you're not planning to have any intercourse soon, you should start training the sooner the better. That doesn't mean you'll haste the moment, the same as carrying condoms in your bag doesn't mean you're looking for sex all the time. It's just a question of getting ready, just in case.

Maybe you think it's too late and you're too much old, even near menopause, so you'll never have intercourse nor children. You'll probably never get pregnant at a certain age but nowadays you can have a child by insemination. Also, you never know when that special man will get to your life. In fact, you don't need any special man, just someone you feel attracted to. Did you ever hear it's never too late for starting doing exercise? The same goes for your vagina, as it's just a muscle. It's never a useless thing. You'll feel happy to overcome the challenge. You'll feel more confident in your daily life. And if you don't get it, you can try again and again for the rest of your life, taking a further step every time.

-This is not for me. I can live without an elastic vagina

You have all the right to think that way, but you have nothing to lose if your vagina gets a bit more elastic. Sometimes women get surgery through their vagina because it's easier, so it's an option you couldn't choose if you had to.

-I don't have time for this

Well, that's the common excuse and you know you're fooling yourself. When something is important for us we do whatever it takes to get it. And there's nothing more important than having your body in the best possible conditions.

-That won't work for me

In the worst possible scenario, you won't be able to

insert even a single finger. But at least you'll get to know how to relax, you'll spend some time getting to know your body better, you'll reflect on your own needs, etc. So you'll get some improvement, in short. And maybe you'll try again with more energy and enthusiasm in the future.

-I don't have a boyfriend so I don't have to worry yet

You don't have him now but you'll have one some time, or maybe you're just avoiding men unconsciously. Anyway, the sooner you work this out, the better. Don't wait until you have a partner, because your problem will become his problem too, and it's stressful for you and unfair for him, although he should support you.

-Training my vagina makes me feel like a weirdo

You may look at it this way: all sexually active women train their vaginas constantly by the intercourse with their partners or by themselves. Women of a certain age usually train their vagina muscles to tone them up, using the Kegel exercises. So you'll be training a certain part of your muscles, it's not weird at all.

Anyway, if you're reading this book it means you want to take a step forward, or to try at least, so I don't need to encourage you anymore. Let's see now the essential part in your path to having a normal vagina: how can you stretch it?

My vaginal exercises

I'll tell you how I stretched my vagina, gradually. This is important, you have to take it easy. If you feel you're hurting yourself, your brain will make you feel blocked so you can't go on. Before inserting anything, you have to realize if you're contracting your pelvic muscles. If it's the case, stop tightening. The first times you have to be totally relaxed. Get a good massage or choose a moment of full relax. Maybe after having a bath or when you're awakening. Look for a comfortable place where nobody can disturb you. You can lie down in bed or sit on a bath. Start by massaging your pubis and then the entrance to your vagina. When you feel at ease, insert your finger after you lubricate it. You don't have to do anything else for a while. Use just one finger and don't move it. Just leave it there. The point is getting used to the sensation. You'll soon be able to move it a little, gently. You can do this as a part of your relaxing routine. There's no need to do it daily if you don't want to. It has to be something easy, not a stressing issue. You can do it a couple of days a week and then try to take a step further. When you practice for a while you won't need so much previous preparation and you'll get further in less time. Until there comes a time when you just check you can easily insert a few fingers for some seconds. That's how I keep the habit and train the elasticity. If you spend some time without training, don't worry: start from the beginning again.

When I could only insert one finger, sometimes I did the exercise while I masturbated, touching my clitoris as well. I remember my vagina was so hardened that my finger hurt because when I had an orgasm, all the muscles contracted and my finger was trapped in there. And a finger has a bone inside, so we can guess what a penis could feel under such pressure.

You can train any time or when you feel horny. It's not a bad idea, because you connect the exercise to something pleasurable, and also, your vagina can stretch more easily when you're excited.

When you feel comfortable with the first finger, your battle against vaginismus is almost won. The vagina is a fascinating muscle. Its elasticity is amazing. Just think when a woman gives birth to a baby. And because it's a muscle, it can stretch and contract too.

The key is getting to stretch it at a good pace for you and it's only up to you to decide on that. Maybe you use one finger for a year before you try your second, or maybe you try your second after a month. The important point is to make some progress. Don't hurry, don't do the foolish things I did.

So the first finger is the most important, it's the step which starts a long road. After that, it's just a matter of time and practice. Explore your vagina at your pace, you'll just see it reacts to the exercise. When you get used to having one finger inside, start to move it gently. You'll find hardened muscles at first, obviously. It's just for the lack of practice. Touch the spot where you feel it's tightened and massage there. After a few seconds, while you relax all your body, you'll notice the spot relaxing too. Do it slowly and use only the tip of your finger. You can press against the walls if you feel at ease. There's not much room towards the pubic bone. The back part, towards the rectus, is usually softer. The side parts are not so soft. When you get to loosen those parts you'll have done a great job.

When I could insert two fingers, I realized something important. The vagina can adjust to the shape of the object you insert, but it always remains a bit rounded or cylindrical. I mean, when you insert two fingers, there's still some room left. So you can move your fingers gently to check the elasticity of the walls. This is the big difference between my method and the expensive dilators. If you can insert the smallest dilator, that doesn't mean you can insert the next one. Because you can't push gently the vaginal walls with a dilator. But you can do it with the tip of your finger! So when you're able to insert one finger, try to stretch your vagina, pressing against the back part and the sides.

At first, everything is hard. In my case, hard as a rock. I thought it was impossible it could get softer someday. But if you press gently with a finger, slowly, carefully, relaxing at the same time, I promise you: the muscle loosens up. It's the same thing when your neck or your shoulders are tense and you get a massage. So little by little, your vagina will relax by the massage and your finger will be able to move inside more easily.

When you're no longer afraid of touching your vagina and you feel confident by your progress, you can press a bit stronger. If you feel like it, use one finger of each hand and push in opposite directions. You can stop when it hurts or you can hold on for a while if you're ready to. It's a good moment for using the anesthetic ointment. And if your hymen breaks, don't panic. For good or for bad, we're used to bleeding during our periods. But you'd better go slowly so you don't have any problem. And go to the doctor if you hurt yourself, of course. I don't encourage you to do some stupid thing, please, take it easy and don't insert the next finger until you feel totally comfortable with the previous step. Don't forget to relax your vagina when your finger is inside, breathing and thinking everything's fine.

The dilators don't allow you to gradually stretch your vagina, as I told you before. And they reach too deep, unlike your fingers. The problem with your fingers is you have to find the right position to insert them. Lying on a bed or in the bath makes it easier, especially when you're inserting three or four fingers. At that point, a penis will probably enter your vagina easily.

The entrance to your vagina is a tricky part. When you insert a finger you realize everything is softer beyond the entrance. You can curve a finger and massage the zone beyond the entrance, trying to stretch it from the inside. Every progress is welcome. It's up to you to find out what works best for your vagina.

In my case, it was helpful to do this: pushing with the finger/s inside so as to make room for the next one. Obviously, you can't insert a penis gradually. So you'll have to practice inserting a few fingers at the same time, once you're able to have them into your vagina. That's when you'll see all the previous training is worth it. You'll place three or four lubricated fingers at the entrance of your vagina and then you'll push. You'll feel the pressure, of course, like it happens on the intercourse, but your fingers will get in easily and you won't feel discomfort because you'll be used to the sensation by then. When you reach that point, you'll be fully ready for the intercourse. I'm sure you'll get it if you try. If someone like me did it, I bet you can do it too.

Final tips

Some women think they must stand the pain on their first intercourse or at any other time. It's sort of a general belief and I think it's awful to think that way. The disinformation can do much harm. We don't know our own body nor how it works, and that's why many women resignedly endure the pain or avoid intercourse and develop vaginismus. You have the right to decide when and how you'll learn about your vagina, please don't surrender to what "normal" standards tell you to do.

The same goes for men. If we don't know our own bodies, they know less. Most of them often watch well-trained vaginas on porn. But many married women have never had intercourse and they keep waiting for a miracle, they hope someday a penis will get into their vaginas somehow, even without a previous warm-up. Or they try the wrong method, like trying it with their partners without training alone first. You don't have to suffer just to please a man. And he may fear to hurt you and become impotent, or he may think you're refusing him.

There's no such thing as "normal sex" or everything is normal in sex, it depends on how you look at it. Forget about the word normal. The only normal thing is you're afraid of getting hurt in a new and unknown experience, and no one can blame you for it. So don't feel guilty or ashamed because your vagina is unlike other women's... yet. Despite some infrequent cases of abnormal vaginas in the need of surgery, the truth is, most the vaginas can be stretched. Yours too. I hope my advice is helpful and thank you so much for reading.

I wish you all the best :)

Printed by Amazon Italia Logistica S.r.l.
Torrazza Piemonte (TO), Italy

16457867R00034